TESTIMONIALS

ON LEADING UNDER PRESSURE...

"**Women Business Enterprises** and business women in general live under all sorts of pressure and perform daily balancing acts. Some of us have developed skills to help us cope with our roles as business and community leaders, mothers, sisters and daughters. Many of us need help - that's where *Leading under Pressure* comes in - **a great resource for us all.** Thanks, Gaby for your insight, your thoroughness and your ability to help us not only define, but refine what we are looking for and what we can expect."

—Nancy Allen, President & CEO, WBDC
Florida Affiliate of the Women's Business Enterprise
National Council

"**Entrepreneurs** rarely have the opportunity to openly discuss the unique stress they experience in their lives. I was very impressed by your ability to **immediately resonate with a group of business owners from around the world.** I truly believe **you made a difference in each of our lives** that day."

—Calvin Carter, Business Owner & EO Member, EO
Regional Director, North America

"Dr. Cora's latest work, *Leading under Pressure* is a crisp, clear, **insightful essential for every senior executive's tool box.** In it, she presents invaluable information drawn from her years in the trenches as a doctor, coach and consultant in a **highly user-friendly and inspirational** manner... a must-read for any manager in today's corporate environment!"

--Cathleen R. Pratt, President & CEO
The Revenue Generators

"In her book *Leading Under Pressure*, Dr. Gabriela Corá depicts and addresses the most important challenges that Executives and Corporate Professionals face in their daily practices. **The content of this book is as useful to the busy business executives as it is to physicians at large,** and especially to psychiatrists and other mental health professionals.

In this text, Dr. Corá demonstrates extremely well **the role of stress and burnt-out vis-à-vis medical and psychiatric conditions.** Obviously, **this book is essential for everyone interested in the topic of health and well-being.**"

--Pedro Ruiz, M.D., President,
American Psychiatric Association

"Gaby's has been a wonderful coach/mentor in working through very difficult family problems in our business. **Her insight into interaction between brothers who are also business partners has been a tremendous help to me** as I have taken brothers and cousins and assigned them to areas where their best talents can be used to move the business ahead without alienating them or causing an impasse."

ON MANAGING WORK IN LIFE...

"Dr. Cora, You gave an amazing presentation at the **Women's Business Network** for the Coral Gables Chamber. We were all touched! I truly felt that you were speaking to me as you touched upon **Trouble at the Top** and **Managing Your Life.** I left that lunch and analyzed my current life/work situation. I went through your seven steps and I can honestly say that **I have been more productive, healthier and happier!** Thank you, Gaby."

"Your New Life Business plan has been a tremendous value in 'redirecting' my life in the manner in which I want it to go versus losing control to life circumstances. After three plus years I am still using it as my foundation to move forward with my daily life. You should spread the word about this great tool that you developed as it will assist many!"

"Dr. Corá - Thank you, your presentation was lively and the concept easy to grasp; **our group appreciated your**

talk on life-work management tremendously!

On a personal note the information was very timely as I've realized that the only way to approach life and work is to **apply your concept of "AIM / IAM."** So I'm consciously making changes in my life that will allow me to maintain focused on what my goals are so that I can accomplish them and enjoy life!!!"

—Ana Alleguez, President & WPO Member,
Alleguez Architecture, Inc.

"First and foremost it was comforting after our initial discussion knowing that we had someone competent to turn to in helping deal with sensitive issues that can arise from time to time. Since these issues can develop rather quickly, the sooner they can be dealt with the better. I was very impressed with Gaby's response time and the cooperation to work around the schedule of all parties involved.

In addition, **Gaby always made everyone feel very comfortable with expressing their feelings or concerns.** All of her advice was always well thought out, and presented in a professional, non-demeaning manner. This could be very difficult to do if you are not an expert in knowing how to **effectively communicate** with people and have the experience in solving tough issues that can come about in businesses. **We felt very fortunate to have met Gaby and made her be part of our team."**

—Terry W. Claus, President
Home Financing Center

ALPHA FEMALE

LEADER OF A
PACK OF BITCHES

"WINNING STRATEGIES TO BECOME
AN OUTSTANDING LEADER."

GABRIELA CORÁ, MD, MBA

LCCN: 2008925677
ISBN: 978-1-933437-09-5

This book was printed in the United States of America.

Cover and Interior Design by:

Prime Concepts Group Publishing (PCG)
Website: www.PrimeConcepts.com
Cover design: Jeff Sparks, PCG
Interior design: Chad Fatino, PCG

We thank Roy Llera Photography for Dr. Gabriela Corá's pictures

Published by:

The Executive Health & Wealth Institute, Inc.
Address: 8101 Biscayne Boulevard, Suite 516, Miami, FL 33138, USA
Telephone: 1-866-762-7632
Website: www.ExecutiveHealthWealth.com
For internet book purchases, please visit:
www.AlphaFemaleBook.com
For bulk orders of this book contact us at:
Resources@ExecutiveHealthWealth.com

CONTENTS

ACKNOWLEDGEMENTS

I would like to dedicate this work to all women from whom I have learned from in my journey: for my teachers, who had all the patience in the world guiding a strong group of female students; to my classmates, who years ago were friends and foes and have now become sisters; to my mothers and sisters, mentors and colleagues, to all my friends.

To all the men who have mentored and guided me, to my bosses, colleagues, clients, and employees. To my husband and son.

I promised Natalia, my daughter, that I would protect her name and future career by not adding her name as an author of this work. Natalia, you are the best of ghost writers, thank you for transcribing my thoughts into each and every written word, adding ideas, pushing me to get this work done, and being the best of positive Alpha Fees in training.

Introduction

"You gain strength, courage and confidence by every experience in which you really stop to look fear in the face. You are able to say to yourself, "I lived through this horror. I can take the next thing that comes along . . . You must do the thing you think you cannot do."

--Eleanor Roosevelt (1884-1962)
"You Learn by Living" (1960)

My goal in writing this book has a specific mission:

- First, to draw insight into the Alpha Female and characterize her description.

- Second, to improve the Alpha Female and her relationship with others.

- Third, to help others survive and improve their relationships with Alpha Females.

This book is partly drawn from personal experience. Growing up in an all-girls school, I'm no stranger to competition. Survival skills were of essence to succeed personally and grow into a group to be able to become a part of the pack. Interestingly, I often found myself polarized during different times going to school when the position of being a positive leader and a negative leader were determined mostly by politics and not always for the greater good.

There are a couple of instances that I would like to relate

3

to you that may explain a little more about my purposes in writing this book. One is a board room situation I experienced where one Alpha Female stated that the problem we were experiencing between several Alpha Females fighting for power seemed to be that these "dog fights" were due to these Alpha Females constantly competing. It was clear to me that there was only one Alpha Female starting fights with every other female in the group.

She feared that all the other females would potentially overthrow her. The men were silent observers of this mess despite being part of the group with supposedly equal say in decision-making. It was pure survival. This was one story that inspired part of the book.

In another experience, also in a board room meeting setting, it was obvious women were a minority but they instigated other women "to be a part of the pack," voting on issues based on "sticking together as women" rather than voting for the best options to resolve specific situations with great impact. This group of women used the "pack mentality" and peer pressure to make themselves leaders with their own benefit in mind.

The spark that lit the fuse of inspiration in me was a recent event honoring successful women in the community and in which I became part of a question/answer session. During the panel discussion, I noted that some women became focused on certain themes, namely family and anti-men sentiments.

When it was my turn to speak, I pointed out that men are not always the problem in advancing our careers, but rather that women sometimes stand in the way of other women. When I mentioned this, the audience had a strong positive reaction (both men and women) although some of my fellow panelists were disturbed by what I'd said. One woman claimed that most of her workforce was women, as a sort of defense, and another woman claimed to disagree entirely but also admitted that she preferred a male boss over a female one.

In another panel, women were advocating for advancing other women in medicine who wanted a part-time position but full-time opportunities and pay so that they could be stay-at-home moms as well as full-time expert doctors. In this case, I also spoke up that a man or woman who wished to work twice as many hours and who was producing twice as much work deserved, in fairness, greater opportunities and more pay simply because they were doing more quality work.

Needless to say, angry female laser eyes tried to disintegrate me, although inevitably, silent men came in private to thank me for a point they would not dare make this day and age. I believe this is another reason this book had to be written – many men are thinking it, but only a woman could say what I am about to say.

The goals of this work are to draw insight into the Alpha Female, the positive **(Alpha Fees)** and the negative leaders, which I will state only once are known as Alpha Bitches **(Alpha Fee Bees)**; to improve true respect and draw from quality of work and ability to get things done rather than opportunistic abuse of power.

Another goal is to look at the relationship between an Alpha Female and those around her as well as finding survival tips for men and women, trying to improve this relationship so that everyone can do their best. Finally, my goal is to help Alpha Females reach their true potential as great leaders and not fall back on being just opportunistic parasites who feed off of the grief of others in order to get ahead. Please note, all Alpha Fee Bees need to do to reach their full potential is to "drop" the Bee!

"You must do the thing you cannot do..."

The first step to achieve this state is to want to **change.** The next step is to establish a **plan** for change and improve. The third is to **implement the plan** and grow stronger.

It is that simple. The good news is I do not know any Alpha Fee Bee who is truly happy, unless she has built an impenetrable tower where she stands alone. Not having any open channel of communication with the outside world, makes it tough even if the Alpha Female tells the world that she's better alone than in bad company.

Needless to say, I was also inspired by Cesar Millán, who is not only knowledgeable of the psychology of dogs but an intuitive master of the psychology of people. His mission is to rehabilitate dogs and train people to help create a strong pack leader. My mission is to assist people achieve their maximum potential for their own benefit and for the benefit of society.

This book is meant to draw smiles on everybody's faces. If you see yourself frowning upon what you read, read again, and see if there is any truth in what is being expressed. If you don't see any truth in this work, stop reading, this book is not meant for you, don't waste your time. On the other hand, if you find yourself smiling, giggling, or laughing out loud, keep reading. I hope you find this book amusing and hope it will make a difference in the way you live your life. With the best of intentions,

Gabriela Corá, MD, MBA

Miami Shores, Florida, 2008.

LET'S GET STARTED

ARE YOU AN ALPHA FEE OR AN ALPHA FEE BEE?

Rate yourself in each of these questions and add up at the end.

Never	Rarely	Sometimes	Often	Always
1	2	3	4	5

1. I like to be in charge

1	2	3	4	5

2. People say I like to be in charge

1	2	3	4	5

3. I am in charge

1	2	3	4	5

4. People say I am in charge

1	2	3	4	5

5. I am a born leader

1	2	3	4	5

6. I lead because I am supposed to lead

1	2	3	4	5

7. I like to work in teams where others complement my capabilities

1	2	3	4	5

8. I like to work in teams only if I am in charge

1	2	3	4	5

9. I don't like to work in teams

1	2	3	4	5

10. I don't like to work in teams because I end up doing all the work

1	2	3	4	5

11. No one works as hard as I do

1	2	3	4	5

12. I enjoy giving orders

1	2	3	4	5

13. I am bossy

1	2	3	4	5

14. People say I am bossy

1	2	3	4	5

15. People do what I ask them to do because they
    respect me

1	2	3	4	5

16. People do what I ask them to do because they fear
    me

1	2	3	4	5

17. I get people to do things for me by pretending to be
    their friend

1	2	3	4	5

18. I get people to do things for me by leading a joint
    vision of what needs to get done

1	2	3	4	5

19. I feel secure in my position of power

1	2	3	4	5

20. People are constantly trying to take my position of power

1	2	3	4	5

21. There's a lot of chaos at work

1	2	3	4	5

22. Work is organized and efficient

1	2	3	4	5

23. I talk about others at work behind their back

1	2	3	4	5

24. I only speak about others if I have something good to say about them

1	2	3	4	5

25. No one but me does the job

1	2	3	4	5

26. If I'm not at the office, everything falls apart

1	2	3	4	5

27. I encourage others to be independent and resolve issues on their own

1	2	3	4	5

28. I ask my employees to always check with me before doing their job

1	2	3	4	5

29. I trust my employees' good judgment at work

1	2	3	4	5

30. I mind my own business

1	2	3	4	5

31. I get jealous if my boss compliments someone else

1	2	3	4	5

32. Men are promoted more than women

1	2	3	4	5

33. I prefer to have a male boss

1	2	3	4	5

34. Women and minorities are promoted more often than men

1	2	3	4	5

35. I prefer to have a female boss

1	2	3	4	5

36. I don't have a preference in regards to my boss' gender, I just want them to be good

1	2	3	4	5

37. I want to follow a boss who is a leader

1	2	3	4	5

38. I want a boss I can manipulate

1	2	3	4	5

39. When I want to advance in my career, I make myself strong

1	2	3	4	5

40. When I want to advance in my career, I bring down my competitors

1	2	3	4	5

41. I use the fact that I'm a woman to advance in my profession or career

1	2	3	4	5

42. I use the fact that I'm a man to advance my career

1	2	3	4	5

43. I use my looks to advance in my career

1	2	3	4	5

44. I stay out of the workplace politics

1	2	3	4	5

45. I create workplace politics

1	2	3	4	5

46. I prefer to follow someone else's lead

1	2	3	4	5

47. I avoid conflict at all cost

1	2	3	4	5

48. I ignore conflict

1	2	3	4	5

49. I love to create conflict at work

1	2	3	4	5

50. I resolve conflict

1	2	3	4	5

51. When I argue I point out the problems at stake and strive to resolve them

1	2	3	4	5

52. When I argue, I get personal to win

1	2	3	4	5

53. I like to win arguments

1	2	3	4	5

54. I don't mind losing arguments if I'm wrong

1	2	3	4	5

55. When arguing, I strive to find a midpoint

1	2	3	4	5

56. I strive for the improvement of my group

1	2	3	4	5

57. I work hard to advance myself

1	2	3	4	5

58. I get along well with most of my colleagues

1	2	3	4	5

59. Everyone around me is inefficient

1	2	3	4	5

60. I stand alone

1	2	3	4	5

61. People don't get it

1	2	3	4	5

62. I accept feedback from my boss

1	2	3	4	5

63. My boss is a jerk

1	2	3	4	5

64. I accept feedback from colleagues

1	2	3	4	5

65. I accept feedback from my employees

1	2	3	4	5

66. I appreciate others' points of view

1	2	3	4	5

67. I prefer to promote men

1	2	3	4	5

68. I prefer to promote other women

1	2	3	4	5

69. I'm glad when the right person is promoted

1	2	3	4	5

70. I dislike when a strong woman is promoted

1	2	3	4	5

71. I fear other women who are more capable than I am

1	2	3	4	5

72. I help those who deserve to get promoted

1	2	3	4	5

73. I make it difficult for others to get promoted

1	2	3	4	5

74. I dislike having others make more money than I make

1	2	3	4	5

75. I am moody

1	2	3	4	5

76. People say my mood is up and down

1	2	3	4	5

77. People think I am Dr. Jekyll and Mr. Hyde

1	2	3	4	5

SCORE

If you had high scores in items 1, 2, 3, 4, 5, 7, 12, 14, 17, 18, 21, 23, 26, 28, 19, 35, 36, 38, 43, 49, 50, 52, 53, 54, 55, 56, 57, 61, 63, 64, 65, 68, and 71, chances are, you are an **ALPHA FEE!**

Alpha Fees are strong, positive leaders who enjoy being in charge yet are great team-players and enjoy establishing win-win situations. They appreciate good challenges and strive to win by doing their best. They mind their own business and have consistently advanced in their position of power. Their battles are fair: they win out of their own merit. Both men and women respect these alphas, as they know they will always bring the greater good to the center of focus rather than any personal gain.

These alphas have a distinct personality. They are easily distinguishable from their pack. They stand tall and are direct in their style; they "walk the walk and talk the talk." They are trusted for their word and their employees will follow their lead with ease. Their environment is harmonious and they will help their employees shine and become stronger, even if that means their employees could take their position. Alpha Fees share their positive energy with their loved ones, at work and with their employees. They are well respected by their family members, friends, employees, colleagues, and friends.

ALPHA FEES – Cheat Sheet

1. Good leaders
2. Encourage others to succeed
3. Develop talents in others, even if others will outshine them
4. Takes care of herself and others along the way
5. Looks at the greater good instead of self-benefit
6. Focuses on task, minimizes emotional stake
7. Creates alliances to get the job done
8. Well-respected by others
9. They "walk the walk and talk the talk"
10. Networks – excellent communicator

If you had high scores in items 1, 2, 3, 4, 6, 8, 9, 10, 11, 13, 15, 16, 19, 20, 22, 24, 25, 30, 31, 32, 37, 39, 40, 42, 44, 46, 47, 48, 51, 52, 58, 59, 60, 62, 62, 66, 67, 69, 70, 72, 73, 74, and 75, 76, and 77, chances are, you are an **ALPHA FEE BEE!**

Alpha Fee Bees seem to be strong on the outside but they are weak on the inside. They are negative leaders who enjoy being in charge for fear of being in someone else's charge. Many Alpha Fee Bees believe they are good leaders, yet they don't work well with others and boycott initiatives where others will shine, even if the initiative will benefit the organization. They always try to secure their position of power and prefer to win alone rather than everybody win. They fear good challenges and strive to win by attacking their opponents' weaknesses.

They mind others' business rather than their own and they tend to criticize everyone around them: no one is as good as they are, they think. They lead by manipulating their employees and their bosses. They prefer male bosses (in fear they would have a woman boss like themselves). They are moody and emotional in their approach and they will get personal in arguments. These Alphas will only implement initiatives if they can have direct personal gain. People follow their orders out of fear and will keep their distance to survive. Their environment is chaotic, with plots of stabbings behind the back at all levels. Alpha Fee Bees say they "have to" do what they do to survive: it's a tough world out there. Alpha Fee Bees drain energy from the workplace: they are inefficient with managing their time and others' time and this will manifest in each and every area of their life.

ALPHA FEE BEES

1. Operate by fear and manipulation
2. Spend more time trying to stay in power than getting the job done
3. Waste time trying to be liked
4. Put down those around her
5. Plot to get on top at all costs
6. Self-centered and fearful of others' plotting to take her job
7. Project negativity to others trying to out-throw her and uses this as an excuse to defend herself
8. Insecure about her position
9. Try to establish emotional alliances
10. Say she "must" be this way to gain the respect of others

And the DELTAS wag behind...

Delta females and males will follow both Alpha Fees and Alpha Fee Bees' leads. While Alpha Fee followers may become great players in their organizations, Alpha Fee Bee followers will go on survival mode: they'd rather play ghost rather than stretch their necks, avoiding a direct attack to their jugular. Stay tuned for our next books of this series!

CHAPTER 1

PUPS IN TRAINING

Culture dictates that girls are cute, dress in pink, play with dolls, and play nice. They are supposed to be easygoing and avoid conflict or confrontation at all costs. Alpha Females are born into cultural structures with well-set expectations. Parents enable this attitude and the presence of other siblings at home, whether boys or girls, will further impact this role.

If a girl is born into a family with sons, the girl will be exposed to more masculine activities but she will be encouraged to undertake female-related play and activities. Not much of another role except to play with dolls when she is young: smooth, gentle, and kind. Boys of the same age will be expected to play with different toys, be rougher, wrestle, or be more mischievous. Remember, this is all stereotype and not a set-in-stone rule for how women should be raised or even how women have been raised. If this young girl likes more action-driven activities, society will label her a "tomboy."

When this girl goes to school, the strong social message is to play nice with the other kids (she is not supposed to play rough), and she is expected to participate in play with other girls. Tomboys don't follow these roles and often play more like boys and with boys. Many tomboys have grown to become Alpha Fees. This is part of the dichotomy: the young girl who was meant to play nice, wearing pink, and playing with dolls now starts participating in sports where the competitive nature of the activity prevails. Her parents now encourage her to run fast, kick a ball, be savvy in gaining a ball from her opponent, and score. Remember, the woman is still expected to be ladylike and sweet outside of the sports arena but during game time, girls must be aggressive and competitive to gain their team's, teachers', coaches', and parents' acceptance.

As the girl continues to grow, those who start excelling in academics will probably devote more time than guys to improve their studies (again, this is only a stereotype and not true of every single girl out there). When young women are ready for college, the new freedom unleashes a new side of the young woman. No parents are around to stop her now from acting out, experimenting with everything. Yet, there is always the dilemma and mixed role of independence: family vs. career. It seems that women cannot bake their cake and eat it too: either they will develop a wonderful career or have children and devote themselves only to this venture.

Women who manage to have a great career and build a solid family at the same time are labeled as "superwomen." Some will criticize them as bad mothers because they will argue these women cannot possibly devote themselves completely to their children. It is often other women who give "superwomen" the harshest criticism. Generation Y (the younger generation), appreciates life choices which do not demand 24/7 work, both for young men and women. However, some of the expectations do not integrate with the intense work ethics of the career paths they choose.

For instance, I met a young medical doctor fresh out of school who wanted to become a prominent surgeon with all the attached benefits and career opportunities. She also wanted to devote only one day a week to her surgical career. For a well-trained surgeon in practice, either male or female, reaching for the top of this demanding career would mean constant practice and improvement of skills, which would be impossible to attain in a one-day-a-week practice. "Superwoman" doesn't just happen. No matter how skilled the woman, there are always sacrifices.

Alpha Fees with school-age kids will enhance their children's talents, helping them find their best abilities by nurturing and encouraging their development, even if the parent is busy in their work or in their careers. The presence of the Alpha Fee mother will be obvious. Alpha Fee Bees will, instead, live vicariously through their kids, pushing them to follow the career paths they themselves wish they'd undertaken at the same age. Envy and criticism of others could prevail, enhancing the child's feeling of inadequacy and inferiority. The young will feel this pressure and this criticism of others will prevail: it's easier to see the fault in the neighbor rather than concentrate on making oneself stronger.

CHAPTER 1: LESSONS LEARNED

1. Make sure you are not giving conflicting messages. As parents, be consistent. Enhance your alpha's training in all areas: help them be strong in academics while they are growing up, encourage the development of their talent, and their participation in group sports when they are young. Watch out if you are demanding they behave as demoiselles in social situations and as savage beasts in a soccer game.

2. When your girl comes home bickering about what this or that girl said to her, encourage her to get the criticism out of her system and help her switch into a more positive activity. Encourage her to solve her difficulties with others, give suggestions, but help her handle it on her own. Make it clear the expectation is not for her to obsess about this issue but that your expectation is for her to resolve it. Don't encourage the criticism; avoid making negative remarks about others.

3. If you see your young girl is already plotting against others, help her shift this negative attitude into one in which she can mind her own business and develop her forte. The stronger she becomes, the less others can get under her skin.

4. If your Alpha Fee pup is a born positive leader, encourage her to be understanding and patient with the rest of the world. Encourage activities in which she is not always the leader and praise her for her excellent leadership qualities as much as you praise her for collaborative attitudes.

5.   Avoid "overprotecting" your girl from outside criticism. Let her learn how to handle it. If you don't, you will be giving her the message that you don't believe she can handle it on her own.

6.   Praise both boys and girls for their good qualities. Avoid making comments of one or the other being assertive, strong, studious, capable, talented, or athletic based on their gender.

7.   Help your girl become assertive from a young age. Encourage her to clarify her thoughts and give her time to finish her thought process in a discussion. Assist her in focusing on the task to be discussed.

8.   When you need to point out issues you feel your child needs to resolve, focus on the issue itself and avoid making personal comments.

9.   Observe how others treat your girls. You may want to communicate more positive ways of encouragement with your girl's teachers and coaches.

10. Make sure you are an excellent role model. The apple doesn't fall far from the tree.

CHAPTER 2

LET'S BLAME IT ALL ON MEN

Men make more money than women. Men get better jobs. Men get better options. Men negotiate for their job salaries better than women do. Ever since a girl is growing up with a tumultuous brother, the message for her is be patient, be kind, boys are just that way. Little girls learn to be patient with their male counterparts.

Boys will out-speak girls in class, so much so that nowadays they're even told they cannot raise their hands unless some girls have a turn to speak up first. Boys are known to be more impatient and are thought to be less mature and there are many preconceptions that women have carried to their workplaces. Anywhere from that men are more interested and ambitious in advancing their careers regardless of the consequences, that they will confront others directly, and that they are more assertive.

In general, men advance faster than women in their careers. Men seem to have more opportunities, they take jobs that demand higher risk and many men work more days and/or longer hours than women. Many times men take jobs that women would not want or do not dare undertake.

All the above concepts have elements of truth. Yet, many women have taken these thoughts and twisted them and taken advantage of their weak position. Taking advantage of these victimizing thoughts is as serious as stating a beautiful and smart woman may have obtained a job or a promotion because of her looks or favors.

Women continue to be called aggressive whenever they're trying to make a point, instead of assertive, whereas a man will be called aggressive only if he is about to strike someone else. Women are expected to be quieter than men, or at least not to object like their male counterparts. On the other end, many truly aggressive women are now not shut up by men in a board meeting, even if the behavior of these women is inappropriate, for fear of being perceived as "chauvinistic" or a harasser. Lack or fear of candor makes it harder to address the exploits of Alpha Fee Bees.

When we need to defend our position, it may be expected that women will do this in a subtle way to comply with cultural norms. It may be easier to blame it on men or let men think they can do it in a more aggressive way, rather than allowing ourselves as women to be more assertive and just live with it. When making a point effectively, many women are referred to as "feisty" for being outspoken. Recognizing the appropriate contribution of ideas is paramount in the workplace. It is important to allow for different styles of discussion as long as there is consideration of others' time and a clear understanding of the need to find solutions to a problem or challenge.

I was once invited to an international program representing an American group. The projector went off when it was my time to present our group's conclusions. Our European hosts were shocked to see that a young American woman could give a focused, straight to the point, assertive presentation because this "was a quality that only men had." They did not intend to insult me with their observation but rather meant to compliment me. I graciously smiled and said that many women in the United States are trained to be assertive in their presentations. Internally, I was gnashing my teeth but I understood that this was a culturally accepted fact and I was a strange fish.

All these preconceived cultural notions have persisted through time and many view men as the root of all evil rather than feeling comfortable and insightful about finding their inner strength and talent. This is a projection on others: blaming others for not being able to find better jobs and better situations, when in fact if we are really secure in our position, we would build that strength instead of blaming our mishaps on an easy target.

Let's face it; chauvinism still exists in the world today. Men will put women down and men will try to stop women from rising in their position. However, this is not always the case and the fact is no woman has to put up with that kind of a position anyway. Why should anyone put up with a job where he or she is not treated well? In fact, in many instances, I have observed other WOMEN in charge capping career opportunities for other women!

Now I can hear the men cheering silently in the background and the feminist women preparing the torches and pitchforks. Before we go too crazy, let me explain. Many women in power will still prefer to have a male boss, probably to exploit (charm) her boss of opportunities, whereas Positive Alpha Fees will create strong alliances and a healthy work environment regardless of who is in charge or who is working for her. It isn't a matter of gender; it's a matter of who is getting the job done.

For instance, I have heard in many different instances of women advocating for equal opportunities with their professional male counterparts, striving to receive the same opportunities as men, although they may be wanting to work on a part-time basis. Although statistics still show that women are being paid less than men, let's not upset the balance. If I prefer to work 8 hours a day in order to spend more time with my children and my fellow counterpart works 16 hour days to forward a research career, in all fairness he or she should naturally advance farther than me and be paid more simply because he or she is doing more work. This is not to say that men should be paid more than women, but only that for equal work, there should be equal reward.

Now, I know I'm making even more enemies, but we have to look at the other side of the spectrum as well. There are women in charge who will only advance other women, regardless of their résumé or work ethic and based solely on the fact that they have XX chromosomes. As much as I dislike this trait of a man choosing another man to be in charge, in all fairness, I equally disagree with a woman doing the same thing. Unfortunately, men have taught us this unpleasant practice and we have caught on to it well. Let's face it; if we want equal rights, we've got to play fair.

CHAPTER 2: LESSONS LEARNED

1. Women and men should have equal opportunities to advance in the workplace based on merit and regardless of gender.

2. Women and men should be paid the same amount for the same amount of work.

3. Women and men should both be appreciated for their assertiveness. Remember, if no one else sees the elephant in the room but you, maybe you should be the one to open everyone's eyes to the obvious.

4. It sucks when a man promotes another man when you deserved the position but are, unfortunately, a woman. Let's stop the negative cycle and lead by example.

5. Watch out for your own body language and communication style with male or female employees. Make sure that you are not enabling these differences in communication with your employees.

6. Avoid using stereotypes about both men and women, since this only leads to perpetuating these challenging issues.

7. When you discuss an issue to be resolved, stay focused on the issue. Avoid any personal connotations.

8. Avoid gender stereotypes including "woman-to-woman" positive comments. This will help you remain objective.

9.   If you want to work on a part-time basis to fulfill
     your needs of personal time and work, do not expect
     a similar career advancement and compensation as
     compared to others who work and/or produce three
     times more than you do. Of course, if your work is
     outstanding and you perform and produce as highly
     or even more than your counterparts, you may very
     well deserve the promotion (except if the demands
     are such that you are expected to devote full-time
     attention to the position).

10. Stop thinking about what would happen if you were
     a man! Focus on developing your abilities to the max,
     to become as efficient as you can, and to produce the
     highest quality of work. If you outshine everyone,
     gender won't matter.

CHAPTER 3

HORMONES RULE

Hold on to your hats, ladies and gentlemen, I can already hear the men shifting in their seats and getting a little nervous. After all, they have been trained to stay away from moms, spouses, daughters, or girlfriends during THAT time of the month. Women with PMS may have experienced symptoms ever since their early teens until their menopause. You know exactly what I'm talking about, don't you?

Some women have even proudly displayed their coffee mugs with "Stay Away, I'm having PMS" (now known as PMDD, or Premenstrual Dysphoric Disorder).

To deny a woman's hormone cycle is to deny nature. Male brains ARE different from female brains. It is more socially acceptable to have a woman scientist say this than a male university president say that women are not as mathematically inclined as men, costing him a prestigious position, even if there is some truth to this statement.

Prominent neuroscientists and researchers will avoid this discussion in public for fear that it could be misconstrued by the public. Nobel prize-winning researchers have lost grace for their candor. It seems to be socially acceptable to say this if the person is of the same gender, age, demographic, or sexual orientation of the critique that is to be addressed.

It is a fact that males dominate in jobs that require pure spatial ability and mathematical reasoning, as in actuaries and engineers. However, if equal spatial ability exists, then some females may perform at a higher level. The traditional male description includes independence, aggression, and the provider-hunter role. The traditional female identity, on the other hand, describes her dependence, ability to create intimate connections, relatedness, passivity, and her nurturer-gatherer role.

This does not mean that women are hopeless with numbers or that men are completely incapable of communication. This only means that the majority of women tend to be more communication-centered and men tend to be more mathematically-inclined. Again, this does not apply to everyone and is only a general finding. A more integrative and assertive partnership is appropriate.

Occasionally, PMS will be used as an excuse for bad behavior. Women with PMS can anticipate the more hypersensitive time and prevent episodes of uncalled-for fury. The bottom line is, if you are a Jekyll and Hyde, seek for help! Save the world (from you)!

If you do have PMS and are not treating it, and if it is impacting on your decision-making, both at home and at work, do seek for help, as this is indeed a treatable condition. If your boyfriend or husband is moving out every month, if you are bitching, barking, and biting those around you during that time of the month, you may want to consider this option both for yourself and to save your pack.

Now, if your tendency is to stay moody all month long or to have mood swings with dangerous ups and downs, you may notice your pack avoiding you and hiding at the first sight of you, not knowing if you'll be in a good or bad mood. Seek for professional help. Discuss this with your doctor and with your business coach. Not doing anything about this will negatively impact your position in power, as you will lose respect from everyone around you, including bosses and employees, particularly because they won't know where to stand or where to stand out of your way.

Unfortunately, creating these unstable environments will always have a negative impact in everyone's ability to follow your lead, to plan their work, and to complete their projects. In the extreme, these mood swings will intensify, you will be seen as an Alpha Fee Bee who is narcissistic, self-centered, and paranoid, in fear that she will be overthrown from her position. As discussed earlier, no one needs to overthrow her because she will do this all on her own, but not without damaging the workplace, her colleagues, and employees.

If you believe you are an Alpha Fee and that you become an Alpha Fee Bee two weeks of the month, seek for help! With help, you will hopefully be a consistent Alpha Fee, for the sake of the world!

CHAPTER 3: LESSONS LEARNED

1. Pay attention to your behavior. Everyone else will.

2. There are neurobiological differences between men and women. This is a fact.

3. We think, feel, and act in an aligned way. Remember: our thoughts are expressed verbally and manifested in actions. If we are clear in our thought process, this will be translated clearly when we talk and with our behavior. If our thoughts are disorganized, your speech and behavior will reflect the disorganization.

4. Mood swings are treatable. It is important you take over and do something about this. The impact of your swings will affect you personally, your family, and your organization.

5. If you operate by fear, paranoia, and narcissism, seek for help. You will fall from your position and not necessarily by the work of others. It's just a question of time.

6. Realize it will be more difficult (if not impossible) to rebuild your trust connection with your employees and bosses if you have impaired the relationship to the point of no return.

7. Even if you have severed relationships at work, it is never late to improve.

8. Avoid using cycle mood swings as an excuse to be an Alpha Fee Bee and expect people to put up with your

behavior. It is not good for you and it is not good for the rest of us.

9. Remember: seeking for help is a service to you and to your workforce and organization.

10. PMS (PMDD) is a treatable condition. So is Bipolar Disorder (or Manic Depressive illness). Consult your primary care physician, a psychiatrist, or gynecologist. Treatment may consist of one or a combination of psychotherapy, medication therapy, and lifestyle strategies.

CHAPTER 4

MARKING YOUR TERRITORY

Regardless of whether you are moving up the ranks from cheerleading to class president, captain of your sports team, or head of your debate team, women have opportunities for growth throughout their life cycle.

Girls learn fast. How do we learn to mark our territory? By observing other girls, other females at home and school, and especially by observing other Alpha Fees. If we look up to Alpha Fees at a young age, we will hopefully learn the good skills of being a positive leader and the benefits of leading a team to success in a win-win situation. Everyone is looking up to someone and will pick their role models. If you promote a negative environment, putting those around you down and abusing your power, everyone is hurt. If you use your power wisely and encourage those around you, you are helping not only yourself but others as well.

Are Alpha Fees born or made? The legendary question of the chicken or the egg: which comes first? Leadership characteristics have a strong nature (genetic) and nurture (environment) mix, just as much as many other personality human traits. Our ability to focus, our ability to remain flexible in relationships, as well as our emotional and intellectual capabilities have a high genetic component. However, their manifestation will relate to an enabling environment.

If you are committed to becoming a more positive leader and you want to develop better ways of helping others along the way, you can train yourself or allow others to help coach you. Learning right from wrong is an early lesson. Bending the rules or taking advantage of weaker classmates (or colleagues) may be a combination of learned behavior and planned strategy. Alpha Fees will tend not to take advantage of others, even if this means that they will not remain in power, whereas opportunistic Alpha Fee Bees will invade the show, taking advantage of others in weaker positions and making stronger counterparts weaker in order to maintain their power.

Alpha Fee Bees will create chaos in order to advance in the position of power. Although they may seem very pleasant or even servile as employees, they are the ones who become despots when in power in an obvious shift.

Alpha Fee Bees will create negative relationships where fear, putting others down, non-constructive criticism, and plotting behavior prevails as an observed behavioral characteristic. Many may even use the excuse of needing to behave this way in order to get things done: as a need rather than as a choice. Remember, to rule by fear is only a temporary and hurtful solution to a problem that could be solved in a more positive way by using other techniques.

While Alpha Fees are able to accommodate to situations and show flexible ways of being an employee or in a position of power, their leadership abilities are obvious even when they are not the boss. You will easily spot the potential Alpha Fee Bees, as they will be the first to criticize their Alpha Fee colleague in fear they will become their boss. What goes around comes around. Alpha Fee Bees will eventually receive all the negativity that they threw into the workplace.

If feeling threatened, the Alpha Fee Bee may plot to become the "silent assassin" by maneuvering negative gossip to discredit whoever she may perceive as a potential threat to her power. The silent assassin is an Alpha Fee Bee who feels that her territory is threatened by new talent and she then plots to destroy that perceived threat, meaning people. This act of getting rid of the competition only ends up hurting her position.

It doesn't take a genius to realize that if the Alpha Fee Bee is pretending to be my friend today to outcast her opponent, and if I have observed that she has done exactly the same before, it will not take long to do the same thing to me. Interestingly, many people believe in fairy tales. An astute Alpha Fee Bee will pretend favoritisms and fake friendships with others to move up in power, taking advantage of the weak and blinded. In the end, she will betray you just like she betrayed everyone else. Watch out!

I was once a part of a marketing strategy project where we were presented with two options: either slam our competition and invest our funds in destroying their image, or in strengthening our own message and putting our funds into our positive attributes. My clear advice has always been to mind my own business and focus on maximizing the strengths and creating new strengths in my own business instead of focusing negatively in my opponent's mishaps. I know, naïve, but let me assure you, I sleep like a baby at night!

This may sound too familiar. In anticipation of political campaigns, viewers are bombarded with negative messages and mud-slinging personal attacks of one politician against another. And, if it gets rough, then their spouses will join the negative match. In the end, we have no idea what anyone stands for or their opinion on any of the significant and important issues that matter. All we know is in order to destroy their opponent, people start escalating their attacks, until they retrieve and apologize stating peace should prevail. Then, they recreate their strategy to strike again. All we know is that millions of dollars are wasted on senseless image-bashing. This same sort of negative attribute can be compared to the Alpha Fee Bee who uses the same techniques to make her look better.

Needless to say, in the end, the Alpha Fee Bee will end as the lone wolf, sitting on her conquered mountain, feeling that it is her against the world. She will have proven her point, though, that others would wish her demise, that she is better or more important than anyone else, and that she stands better alone than in bad company. So she ends up right. Right and completely alone.

Remember the example in the introduction when the Alpha Female boss felt threatened, she didn't have the better idea than to not allow the other Alpha Females to conduct their jobs properly? Not only did she frustrate others who wanted to get the job done, but her own ability to show superb productivity as the boss backfired. After all, a good boss will show her ability to lead by the degree of performance and productivity she is able to enhance in those she leads. What does this say about her ability as a leader if at the end of the day, everyone is miserable and nothing has been accomplished?

CHAPTER 4: LESSONS LEARNED

1. Alpha Fees earn their territory. Alpha Fee Bees plot to steal it.

2. If you want to succeed as a positive Alpha Fee, create your strengths in your own abilities and your capabilities in doing the job.

3. Beware of the silent assassin; avoid becoming one.

4. Create a great strategy to conduct your work.

5. Do NOT look at lines of territory but, instead, create strong alliances with complimentary talent. Turf wars do not lead to successful enterprises.

6. The best of strategies to keep your territory is in becoming so positive and strong that your competition cannot reach you.

7. Learn to appreciate your colleagues' good work.

8. Help you colleagues become stronger employees. They will respect your space more if they understand their own position.

9. Help your employees become the best that they can become, even if this means the apprentice's capabilities surpass the master's.

10. Remember, what goes around comes around. Give what you would like to get in return. Don't put out energy that you don't want to come back to you.

CHAPTER 5

CAT FIGHTS?

Men don't usually find anything more attractive than being voyeurs to women in a cat fight. Any time there is a confrontation between women, men watch as if in a trance. With good reason! When women clash, it can get ugly.

While many men in power claim that other men seeking their positions will stab them straight in the chest, women may end up stabbing someone in the back while smiling to the world. This is not to say that all women do this, but only that those who rise to power when they destroy the people on their way often do so in sneaky and under-handed ways. Recall the silent assassin, since this stealthy mode demonstrates the female's battle strategy.

I recently joined a group where gossip was spread about me from a woman in power. This gossip was not only misleading but was also potentially damaging to the work environment. As I reviewed my strategy, I decided to first clarify and then to directly confront the female who believed that she was threatened in her power. Caught off-guard, she immediately spoke in a soft, submissive way, as a purring kitten.

This is to say that she dismissed her negative behavior and pretended she never did anything wrong. She further avoided any potential confrontation that would have exposed her overt lying altogether. Giving a cornered cat an honorable exit is a good strategy (and a good survival skill) to avoid the claws of an insecure Alpha Fee Bee.

This is a battle strategy for you, the reader. Understand that to confront the Alpha Fee Bee in this case was necessary because if I had dismissed or ignored the gossip or even addressed it through more gossip, the situation would have remained the same or would have damaged the work environment even more. My second strategy of not cornering the Alpha Fee Bee after addressing the problem to her attention that I was aware of her behavior stopped any potentially vengeful follow-up. You can establish your position of strength by being clear, assertive, and outlining your intent, moving on with what needs to be done rather than getting involved in the emotional attack. Truth-be-told, Alpha Fee Bee will strike back, without a doubt. On the other hand, life is just too interesting to be wasted with this preoccupation. Remember, you have better things to do with your time than let an Alpha Fee Bee's negativity get to you.

Licking your wounds and moving on with your life might be the best of strategies in some instances. Although the Alpha Fee Bee may be interested in continuing a fight or attacking your weaknesses, remember that you are there to get a job done and not to get involved in cat fights. If this means that you swallow your pride and focus on your job, then you have won the battle after all. The negative Alpha Fee Bee will probably continue to fixate on the cat fight, maybe even tempt you to continue fighting with her, but it will be her loss at the end of the day. You are better off minding your own business, doing your work well, and letting go of bad feelings. If you're doing your job and she's not, you still win but the job of the whole organization may not be achieved. Everyone needs to row together.

CHAPTER 5: LESSONS LEARNED

1. Focus on getting the job done.

2. Let the Alpha Fee Bees fight alone. Stay out of cat fights.

3. Avoid creating chaos to stay on top.

4. Create collaborative opportunities.

5. Clean up your work environment. Don't let nasty feelings clog productivity.

6. Don't take personal insults personally (does this make sense)? Remember, you can only be hurt by the words that you give power to.

7. Always keep emotion under control.

8. Choose your battles carefully. Yet, confront inappropriate behavior when necessary.

9. Stay on task and help others realize cat fights prevent the achievement of common goals.

10. Foster collaborative opportunities, finding a good balance between individual achievements and teamwork.

CHAPTER 6

BIOLOGICAL CLOCK IS TICKING: LET'S KICK TAIL

Hormones rule, remember? Successful and driven women, no matter how battle-hardened and tough, will always secretly, somewhere in their soul, want to be mommies. Good mommies. Whether they are single, married, or involved in same-sex relationships, the idea of having a pup (same or different species) will cross their mind. The incredible amounts of energy that these women have dedicated to their work over the years will start shifting in their eager desire to extend their family. This does not mean that every woman is dying to stay up all night caring for a baby or worrying about college tuition. This only means that at some point, almost every woman thinks about having or not having children.

For those women who have successfully focused their energy in getting things done, noticing they cannot control their biological clock to get pregnant right away may add this bodily function as a task to be achieved. Running out of time, many driven Alpha Fees will decide to go in vitro as an easy and practical way of becoming pregnant, making it a "secure strategy" and overlooking the biological and natural ways of their bodies. This does not mean that IVF or alternative ways of extending a family are negative in any way; it just means that many Alpha Fees will list "getting pregnant" as a task to be achieved. Think of a checklist. Some will take a "conceiving vacation," realizing their hectic schedules are not conducive to getting pregnant. Some will decide to have a surrogate mother. While some may be physically unable to bear a child, some want to avoid the nine-month hormone craze and huge belly experience to continue the hectic lifestyle until the baby is born.

The advances of medicine have offered amazing opportunities in all aspects of the health sciences. At the same time, utilizing these advances in a utilitarian way may take away the biological understanding of cycles and rhythms.

Our bodies are designed with an internal clock for a reason. Some older women even have dangerous experiences in trying to get pregnant and in maintaining healthy pregnancies. Our bodies have naturally evolved in such a way that getting pregnant when we are older will naturally increase our potential for medical complications (such as high blood pressure or gestational diabetes) as well as genetic issues, not to mention problems getting pregnant in the first place. Again, this does not mean that all women must have children at the age of twenty. On the other hand, it is a scientific fact that younger ova are healthier than older ova.

We have looked at women who have devoted their lives to their work and who now are looking to start a family. Let us now look at the kind of mother she wants to be. Younger mothers will need to work hard to set priorities to be successful at both raising a joyful family as well as building their career. Alpha Fees who have children later in life must also balance their work with their family life but do not have the same demands as younger mothers, except for the self-imposed, habitual trend of devoting most of their time to work. In this case, making the child a priority will be a feat on its own. While some would think of leaving their pets behind in case of an emergency (i.e.: evacuating in case of a hurricane), nobody in their right mind would think of leaving their kids behind. Many of us wouldn't leave our pets behind either. By this time, Alpha Fees have trained themselves to put work first, even at an unconscious level. Changing this strong habit is not easy.

Alpha Fee Bees may learn good lessons when becoming a mother. Seeing their child suffer from unfair events may either trigger them becoming conspirators on their child's behalf behind the scenes, or learn of the consequences and want to improve to help their child. What about the kick-ass, aggressive Alpha Female at work who becomes a seemingly harmless, doting mother who sometimes treats her children as her next project? In this case, the child becomes an extension of the Alpha Fee Bee and may be used for her own benefit. She will take advantage of having a child and manipulate a boss in needing to take time off, and, at the same time, she will expect a promotion and will fight for it even if her counterpart devoted more time and effort in getting the job done. Remember earlier about being fair? Kids always tip the balance, no matter your superwoman status.

CHAPTER 6: LESSONS LEARNED

1. Hormones rule: there is a biological clock and it's always ticking.

2. Think of priorities ahead of the game. Although you will live through different situations, try to maintain a balanced overview of the whole picture.

3. Understand the laws of nature and use them to your advantage.

4. Be consistent in all aspects of your life: you can be a caring, kick-ass Alpha Fee boss and mom. The two are not mutually exclusive.

5. Realize you will need to accommodate your lifestyle strategies as you age. This does not have to be a negative experience.

6. If you decide to become a mother in your forties, realize your priorities will shift.

7. If you decide to continue to be in power and you want to extend your family, realize you may need to choose to what degree you want to develop each.

8. Even if you work long hours, having a child will need to make you available to them 24/7 (even if you have people caring for them, or if they are in day care, in school, or with a nanny). This is the main difference from having a pet instead of a son or daughter.

9. Remember that the only way that you will establish a

relationship with your child is by nurturing your bond and establishing excellent communication early on. If you believe your teenager is estranged from you, track where the disconnection started. This doesn't happen in 24 hours.

10. Mentor your employees and nurture your pups: remember, employees were pups once too.

CHAPTER 7

MEN WALKING ON EGGSHELLS

Here's the chapter you men have all been waiting for. You didn't think I forgot about you, did you?

Men, in their wisdom, have learned when to stay away from a demanding mom, sister, girlfriend, or wife at that time of the month. You learned the lesson young. When a woman's hormones are raging, the best strategy is to avoid the woman at all costs and, failing to do this, find other ways to survive. You must be thinking "Duh!"

Alpha Males under Alpha Female domain have two options: either clash or submit. Now, what happens when two dragons collide? Who has the bigger fireballs? Explosive confrontation may appear to Alpha Males like the ideal way to prove their dominance, but remember the silent assassin. Remember that women have a different battle strategy than men. If a man decides that an open confrontation is the best way to dominate an Alpha Female, the Alpha Females may appear to submit but watch out. A seemingly docile Alpha Female usually has a trick or two up her sleeve.

Alpha Fee Bees who fear that anyone is trying to steal her power, whether male or female, will not hesitate to create chaos in order to keep a vice grip on her power. This means that if Alpha Males decide to start confrontations, the Alpha Females will find various ways to undermine the Alpha Male's respect. They will not play fair. This could mean your reputation, men!

In order to survive, Alpha Male masters of strategy will disguise their leadership as Delta Males, wagging their tail behind until they too can strike big fireballs to rise in the ranks. Staying away but getting the job done and creating strong strategies around what needs to be done may indeed be the best of strategies to deal with an insecure Alpha Fee Bee. If you are striving for survival, bite your tongue, get the job done, and let your work speak for itself. No one can accuse you of anything if you have proof to back up your worth.

If you are seeking a promotion and this negative Alpha Fee Bee has put a cap on your sea of opportunities, realize your position is temporary. Alpha Fee Bees will bring about their own doom. If you focus on yourself and work hard to finish those tasks designated to you, you will always get to where you need to be, no matter who stands in your way.

It is amazing to see how successful and intelligent men can shift their survival attitude while under the domain of an Alpha Fee Bee and an Alpha Fee. By nature, most of us learn how to adapt and accommodate to challenging situations. Those of us with more experience and understanding of these events will consciously be able to apply great strategies to survive the workplace and thrive at the same time.

Positive Alpha Fees will create strong alliances with Positive Alpha Males (of course, there are Alpha Male pigs, without a doubt!). They will welcome positive mentorship and advice and it will go both ways. You will both benefit from this kind of relationship. If you are a negative Alpha Male in combination with an Alpha Fee Bee, I truly don't know who's going to win, but I can tell you you're both going to lose.

CHAPTER 7: LESSONS LEARNED

1. If you are an Alpha Male working with a Positive Alpha Female, enjoy and maximize your cross-collaboration because you will have the opportunity to do great things together.

2. If you are an Alpha Male coming up against an Alpha Fee Bee, watch out! Use your head and don't get caught in a fireball war. Your diplomacy will work wonders.

3. Concentrate on getting the job done and avoid any potential confrontation. Keep your posture non-threatening, avoid direct eye contact, and speak in a low voice. Remember they can smell fear!

4. Create strong alliances with positive leaders and employees. Although your Alpha Fee Bee boss will hate it, you are thinking short and long term survival.

5. If you will need to stay in a position under an Alpha Fee Bee, wagging your tail for a while will help you survive. I know, you will feel disgusted, but survival is survival. You don't need to go to a far-away island to prove your skills. You can do this at your local workplace!

6. Don't say anything negative about your Alpha Fee Bee boss or plot against her. Remember, she is her own worst enemy. She doesn't need your help.

7. If she is boycotting your work or suggestions, stay put. Write your recommendations or proposals. Look for an opportunity to bring your positive suggestions in a group setting, tactfully.

8. This may sound like you have to submit to an Alpha Fee Bee, and you do. Remember though that this does not mean you should remain quiet in matters of work-related problems and discussion. This only means stay out of the emotional, personal fights that may result from this Alpha Fee Bee.

9. If you are in a position of power and one of your managers is an Alpha Fee Bee, don't let her get away with murder! Many men think they cannot discipline or give feedback upon someone's negative behavior because she is a woman and you may be sued! Concentrate on the work that needs to be done, the quality of the work, and the need for positive cross collaboration. Consult with your Human Resource department if you need to and create a plan to help this person improve her skills for the benefit of your team, your organization, and your quality of life.

10. If you are married to an Alpha Fee Bee... good luck! My best wishes for her wanting to improve and for you to support her improvement.

CHAPTER 8

SIT, GO FETCH, PLAY DEAD

So now you've learned quite a bit about Alpha Fees and Alpha Fee Bees and you have hopefully appreciated the lessons learned. Now you're ready to determine not only if your boss is an Alpha Fee or an Alpha Fee Bee (like you didn't know, right?) but I also want to leave you with a simple strategy for survival, which is to decide when to sit, go fetch, or play dead.

Remember, you're not a dog, but you may feel like one at the end of the day.

Sit: this is one of the most basic commands you can give your dog. Stroke the female ego: sit and wait for orders with a smile. Be attentive to her needs, show that you are waiting for her to give you important orders as she does not seem to expect for you to decide what to do on your own. Sitting and waiting on the alert may be a great strategy if you are feeling you are walking on eggshells, the "damned if you do, damned if you don't" state. Also, because you are waiting for her orders, you are covering all your bases. She can not accuse you of anything as, "I didn't do anything because I was waiting for your command, master, I mean, ma'am," is in effect. Note that this is not brown-nosing, it is purely a survival strategy.

Go fetch: now you have received the order. Move fast, efficiently, and with sharp efficacy. Do what you were asked to do with a smile, pronto. This is an important strategy because the Alpha Fee Bee will not only be pleased by someone finally doing what she asks but also because you will be seen as non-threatening to her position of power. To "go fetch" means to do your job, to complete your given task, and to focus solely on this mission. This does not include personal requests to pick up her laundry, in case you were worried. This is entirely work-related.

If you receive more than one order at a time, do ask which order the Alpha Fee or Alpha Fee Bee wants completed first (yes, even Alpha Fees can be demanding at times). If you receive more than three, ask her to write each down in the order of most importance. This way, you have documented your orders and can show her that you are attentive to her needs, not to mention you can show her later what you were asked to do. This strategy will enable you to have the last word, at home ("yes, honey"), at work ("yes, ma'am"), no nonsense. I must acknowledge the author of these suggestions. His name is Eduardo Locatelli and we have been married for twenty years.

Play dead: if you messed up, this is the order for you! If you messed up because, although you did exactly what she asked you in the order she asked you but things did not result quite as you had planned (or she expected), playing dead until the storm has passed may be the best of strategies for survival.

This means that even if she tries to attack you, you do not respond. Just give your submissive stare, avoiding direct eye contact, looking a little down, drop your shoulders and one even more so as to look smaller than you are, in a non-challenging position. Bite your tongue and don't tell her "I told you so!" This will save you from saying something you may later regret. You may worry about how other colleagues will look at you. Avoid saying anything negative about the Alpha Fee Bee, your strategy is short-term survival, long-term victory. The only one who will end up looking bad in the end is the Alpha Fee Bee.

CHAPTER 8: LESSONS LEARNED

1. **Sit** – wait for your given task.

2. **Go fetch** – focus on your given task. Just do it, à-la-Nike!

3. **Play dead** – disappear into the woodwork until the storm has passed.

CHAPTER 9

SURVIVAL TIPS

We've addressed the most significant issues that characterize positive female leaders (Alpha Fees) and negative female leaders (Alpha Fee Bees). With the best of intentions to help you survive your experience with Alpha Fee Bees and to assist you in the development of great relationships with Alpha Fees, these are some survival tips:

1. Identify (or smell) the Alpha Female type from a distance. Is she an Alpha Fee or an Alpha Fee Bee? If she's an Alpha Fee Bee, what is your degree of hope that she will improve? Is this hope realistic or just wishful thinking? Your senses should be tingling long before you even shake her hand. Trust your gut feeling. This knowledge is not intellectual, pay attention to your instinct.

2. Identify what makes her tick. Is she power hungry? Does she just want to be on top? Does she appear to be a savage Rottweiler or is she an angry Chihuahua? This may be vital for your survival!

3. Create your survival strategy: what are your goals at your job? Are you at your job in a temporary situation or do you have long-term plans to stay at the job? Create both short and long-term plans.

4. If you are under the spell of an Alpha Fee Bee, focus on what needs to get done and not on the emotional wars that she may be starting around you. Stay calm at all

times, even if you feel like an imploding volcano. Work on your verbal skills and body language.

5. Maintain low-emotion at work. This will help you deal with any Alpha Fee Bee. If this means you explode later, let the storm rage and then let it go. Holding a grudge forever will only hurt you in the end.

6. Avoid confrontation on a personal level. Bring your strategy to the greater good, for the benefit of your team, your clients, and for the benefit of your organization. This will help you gain your colleagues' respect and maintain your own. Remember that to make things personal will only get you in trouble.

7. Create positive alliances but watch out for back-stabbing. What goes around comes around.

8. Connect with the Alpha Fee. How can you work together effectively in a way that you can both win and where you are not viewed as a threat? Help her shine, praise her support in public (only if she has supported you, even a little). Remember, praising a lie feels odd, and she will become paranoid, thinking you are manipulating her.

9. Mind your own business. Avoid falling into her trap of becoming her manipulated subject. This will help you keep everybody's respect.

10. Do not plot to bring the Alpha Fee Bee down. She doesn't need your help, thank you very much, and will do this very well on her own.

CHAPTER 10

LET'S PLAY TOGETHER

The bottom line is we are supposed to work together. A one-person show still exists this day and age. However, most of us work in teams, for groups, and for organizations. Most of us either create products or provide for services to many people. It is of essence to learn effective skills to play together for our own benefit and for the benefit of us all. These are some conclusions:

1. Men and women: we are of the same species. Our brains may be different, but we have complimentary qualities. Let's bring them together.

2. You scratch my back, I'll scratch yours. Let's find win-win opportunities.

3. Find talents at work and bring them forward. It is okay for men to have a more mathematical mind and for women to have more expressive talents. Create opportunities to integrate these abilities for the greater good.

4. Read maps AND ask for directions. The point is getting where you need to go with the least possible roadblocks.

5. This isn't the battle of the sexes. Team up! We're all working together.

6. Want a successful marriage? Want meaningful

interpersonal relationships at work? Want successful alliances? Work at it! Just like money doesn't grow on trees, successful relationships don't happen overnight.

7. Maximize your power of alliance, mediation, and collaboration.

8. Train your pups well; lead by example.

9. For men: don't let Alpha Fee Bees walk all over you. We know many Alphas have abused their power. Show you have a backbone. It's the only way to create respect.

10. For women: remember your femininity! We don't need to cut our hair like men and wear androgynous outfits. It's okay to look fabulous and still kick tail!

CHAPTER 11

TIPS FOR ALPHA FEE BEES TO BECOME POSITIVE MOVERS AND SHAKERS

1. Seek help. If you are an unhappy Alpha who projects all fault and evil to others, seek change.

2. Decide whether you will benefit from medical help, psychological, coaching, mentoring, or all of the above. Take action! It is not a sign of weakness to seek help. It is a sign of weakness to ignore your feelings of weakness.

3. It could be that one person is plotting against you, maybe two...but all of them? If one person does not like you, it's okay, if many don't like you, that may be okay too. But if you justify everybody hating you, chances are, it's not them but you! In general, if this is the case, even you may not like yourself. Become your best friend.

4. Establish alliances to win, not plots to overthrow.

5. Become strong by your own deeds, not by finding fault in or weakening others. Discover what you have to offer to the world.

6. Focus on bringing good services and deeds to the world. This should be your driving force.

7. Avoid high emotion in making any personal, professional, or business decisions, particularly if these will likely impact on others (meaning most of your decisions).

8. Train others to become better than you have ever been. Allow yourself to experience the joy of having the apprentice outdo the master. After all, they're only that good because you helped them get there.

9. Use your position of power when you need to call the shots during times of crisis or during times of chaos. Otherwise, encourage open communication and participation of your team.

10. Use joy as your barometer and the friendships and respect from others that you have generated in your path. Nurture the positive attributes of a powerful leader.

11. If you're spending more of your time trying to be liked by others or plotting to overthrow others from their positions, shift to spending more time on getting your own job done.

12. Form strong alliances with those who share your vision and goals. Avoid promoting others based solely on gender or other demographic issues (this goes for men too!).

13. Stay true to yourself. Don't jump on the bandwagon! Remember that you are a powerful Alpha Female and if no one else will state the obvious problem, then it is your job to guide the pack.

14. Just like love and hate are different manifestations of the same spectrum, positive and negative Alpha Females are polarized expressions of the same strong female leader. As in alchemy, negative can be transformed

into positive. If you believe that you can strive for this power of transformation, then there is nothing to stop you from becoming the best Positive Alpha Female that you can be.

Wishing you the best on your path for improvement,

Gabriela Corá, MD, MBA

Miami Shores, Florida, 2008.

CHEAT SHEET

SUMMARY OF LESSONS LEARNED

1.   Make sure you are not giving conflicting messages. As parents, be consistent. Enhance your alpha's training in all areas: help them be strong in academics while they are growing up, encourage the development of their talent, and their participation in group sports when they are young. Watch out if you are demanding they behave as demoiselles in social situations and as savage beasts in a soccer game.

2.   When your girl comes home bickering about what this or that girl said to her, encourage her to get the criticism out of her system and help her switch into a more positive activity. Encourage her to solve her difficulties with others, give suggestions, but help her handle it on her own. Make it clear the expectation is not for her to obsess about this issue but that your expectation is for her to resolve it. Don't encourage the criticism; avoid making negative remarks about others.

3.   If you see your young girl is already plotting against others, help her shift this negative attitude into one in which she can mind her own business and develop her forte. The stronger she becomes, the less others can get under her skin.

4.   If your Alpha Fee pup is a born positive leader, encourage her to be understanding and patient with the rest of the world. Encourage activities in which

she is not always the leader and praise her for her excellent leadership qualities as much as you praise her for collaborative attitudes.

5.   Avoid "overprotecting" your girl from outside criticism. Let her learn how to handle it. If you don't, you will be giving her the message that you don't believe she can handle it on her own.

6.   Praise both boys and girls for their good qualities. Avoid making comments of one or the other being assertive, strong, studious, capable, talented, or athletic based on their gender.

7.   Help your girl become assertive from a young age. Encourage her to clarify her thoughts and give her time to finish her thought process in a discussion. Assist her in focusing on the task to be discussed.

8.   When you need to point out issues you feel your child needs to resolve, focus on the issue itself and avoid making personal comments.

9.   Observe how others treat your girls. You may want to communicate more positive ways of encouragement with your girl's teachers and coaches.

10. Make sure you are an excellent role model. The apple doesn't fall far from the tree.

11. Women and men should have equal opportunities to advance in the workplace based on merit and regardless of gender.

12. Women and men should be paid the same amount for the same amount of work.

13. Women and men should both be appreciated for their assertiveness. Remember, if no one else sees the elephant in the room but you, maybe you should be the one to open everyone's eyes to the obvious.

14. It sucks when a man promotes another man when you deserved the position but are, unfortunately, a woman. Let's stop the negative cycle and lead by example.

15. Watch out for your own body language and communication style with male or female employees. Make sure that you are not enabling these differences in communication with your employees.

16. Avoid using stereotypes about both men and women, since this only leads to perpetuating these challenging issues.

17. When you discuss an issue to be resolved, stay focused on the issue. Avoid any personal connotations.

18. Avoid gender stereotypes including "woman-to-woman" positive comments. This will help you remain objective.

19. If you want to work on a part-time basis to fulfill your needs of personal time and work, do not expect a similar career advancement and compensation as compared to others who work and/or produce three times more than you do. Of course, if your work is outstanding and you perform and produce as highly or

even more than your counterparts, you may very well deserve the promotion (except if the demands are such that you are expected to devote full-time attention to the position).

20. Stop thinking about what would happen if you were a man! Focus on developing your abilities to the max, to become as efficient as you can, and to produce the highest quality of work. If you outshine everyone, gender won't matter.

21. Pay attention to your behavior. Everyone else will.

22. There are neurobiological differences between men and women. This is a fact.

23. We think, feel, and act in an aligned way. Remember: our thoughts are expressed verbally and manifested in actions. If we are clear in our thought process, this will be translated clearly when we talk and with our behavior. If our thoughts are disorganized, your speech and behavior will reflect the disorganization.

24. Mood swings are treatable. It is important you take over and do something about this. The impact of your swings will affect you personally, your family, and your organization.

25. If you operate by fear, paranoia, and narcissism, seek for help. You will fall from your position and not necessarily by the work of others. It's just a question of time.

26. Realize it will be more difficult (if not impossible) to

rebuild your trust connection with your employees and bosses if you have impaired the relationship to the point of no return.

27.   Even if you have severed relationships at work, it is never late to improve.

28.   Avoid using cycle mood swings as an excuse to be an Alpha Fee Bee and expect people to put up with your behavior. It is not good for you and it is not good for the rest of us.

29.   Remember: seeking for help is a service to you and to your workforce and organization.

30.   PMS (PMDD) is a treatable condition. So is Bipolar Disorder (or Manic Depressive illness). Consult your primary care physician, a psychiatrist, or gynecologist. Treatment may consist of one or a combination of psychotherapy, medication therapy, and lifestyle strategies.

31.   Alpha Fees earn their territory. Alpha Fee Bees plot to steal it.

32.   If you want to succeed as a positive Alpha Fee, create your strengths in your own abilities and your capabilities in doing the job.

33.   Beware of the silent assassin and avoid becoming one.

34.   Create a great strategy to conduct your work.

35. Do NOT look at lines of territory but, instead, create strong alliances with complimentary talent. Turf wars do not lead to successful enterprises.

36. The best of strategies to keep your territory is in becoming so positive and strong that your competition cannot reach you.

37. Learn to appreciate your colleagues' good work and use this energy to improve yourself.

38. Help you colleagues become stronger employees. They will respect your space more if they understand their own position.

39. Help your employees become the best that they can become, even if this means the apprentice's capabilities surpass the master's.

40. Remember, what goes around comes around. Give what you would like to get in return. Don't put out energy that you don't want to come back to you.

41. Focus on getting the job done.

42. Let the Alpha Fee Bees fight alone. Stay out of cat fights.

43. Avoid creating chaos to stay on top.

44. Create collaborative opportunities.

45. Clean up your work environment. Don't let nasty feelings clog productivity.

46. Don't take personal insults personally (does this make sense)? Remember, you can only be hurt by the words that you give power to.

47. Always keep emotion under control.

48. Choose your battles carefully. Yet, confront inappropriate behavior when necessary.

49. Stay on task and help others realize cat fights prevent the achievement of common goals.

50. Foster collaborative opportunities, finding a good balance between individual achievements and teamwork.

51. Hormones rule: there is a biological clock and it's always ticking.

52. Think of priorities ahead of the game. Although you will live through different situations, try to maintain a balanced overview of the whole picture.

53. Understand the laws of nature and use them to your advantage.

54. Be consistent in all aspects of your life: you can be a caring, kick-ass Alpha Fee boss and mom. The two are not mutually exclusive.

55. Realize you will need to accommodate your lifestyle strategies as you age. This does not have to be a negative experience.

56. If you decide to become a mother in your forties, realize your priorities will shift.

57. If you decide to continue to be in power and you want to extend your family, realize you may need to choose to what degree you want to develop each.

58. Even if you work long hours, having a child will need to make you available to them 24/7 (even if you have people caring for them, or if they are in day care, in school, or with a nanny). This is the main difference from having a pet instead of a son or daughter.

59. Remember that the only way that you will establish a relationship with your child is by nurturing your bond and establishing excellent communication early on. If you believe your teenager is estranged from you, track where the disconnection started. This doesn't happen in 24 hours.

60. Mentor your employees and nurture your pups: remember employees were pups once too.

61. If you are an Alpha Male working with a Positive Alpha Female, enjoy and maximize your cross-collaboration because you will have the opportunity to do great things together.

62. If you are an Alpha Male coming up against an Alpha Fee Bee, watch out! Use your head and don't get caught in a fireball war. Your diplomacy will work wonders.

63. Concentrate on getting the job done and avoid any potential confrontation. Keep your posture non-

threatening, avoid direct eye contact, and speak in a low voice. Remember they can smell fear!

64. Create strong alliances with positive leaders and employees around you. Although your Alpha Fee Bee boss will hate it, you are thinking short and long term survival.

65. If you will need to stay in a position under an Alpha Fee Bee, wagging your tail for a while will help you survive. I know, you will feel disgusted, but survival is survival. You don't need to go to a far-away island to prove your skills. You can do this at your local workplace!

66. Don't say anything negative about your Alpha Fee Bee boss or plot against her. Remember, she is her own worst enemy. She doesn't need your help.

67. If she is boycotting your work or suggestions, stay put. Write your recommendations or proposals. Look for an opportunity to bring your positive suggestions in a group setting, tactfully.

68. This may sound like you have to submit to an Alpha Fee Bee, and you do. Remember though that this does not mean you should remain quiet in matters of work-related problems and discussion. This only means stay out of the emotional, personal fights that may result from this Alpha Fee Bee.

69. If you are in a position of power and one of your managers is an Alpha Fee Bee, don't let her get away with murder! Many men think they cannot discipline

or give feedback upon someone's negative behavior because she is a woman and you may be sued! Concentrate on the work that needs to be done, the quality of the work, and the need for positive cross collaboration. Consult with your Human Resource department if you need to and create a plan to help this person improve her skills for the benefit of your team, your organization, and your quality of life.

70.   If you are married to an Alpha Fee Bee... good luck! My best wishes for her wanting to improve and for you to support her improvement.

71.   **Sit** – wait for your given task.

72.   **Go fetch** – focus on your given task. Just do it, à-la-Nike!

73.   **Play dead** – disappear into the woodwork until the storm has passed.

74.   Identify (or smell) the Alpha Female type from a distance. Is she an Alpha Fee or an Alpha Fee Bee? If she's an Alpha Fee Bee, what is your degree of hope that she will improve? Is this hope realistic or just wishful thinking? Your senses should be tingling long before you even shake her hand. Trust your gut feeling. This knowledge is not intellectual, pay attention to your instinct.

75.   Identify what makes her tick. Is she power hungry? Does she just want to be on top? Does she appear to be a savage Rottweiler or is she an angry Chihuahua? This may be vital for your survival!

76. Create your survival strategy: what are your goals at your job? Are you at your job in a temporary situation or do you have long-term plans to stay at the job? Create both short and long-term plans.

77. If you are under the spell of an Alpha Fee Bee, focus on what needs to get done and not on the emotional wars that she may be starting around you. Stay calm at all times, even if you feel like an imploding volcano. Work on your verbal skills and body language.

78. Maintain low-emotion at work. This will help you deal with any Alpha Fee Bee. If this means you explode later, let the storm rage and then let it go. Holding a grudge forever will only hurt you in the end.

79. Avoid confrontation on a personal level. Bring your strategy to the greater good, for the benefit of your team, your clients, and for the benefit of your organization. This will help you gain your colleagues' respect and maintain your own. Remember that to make things personal will only get you in trouble.

80. Create positive alliances but watch out for back-stabbing. What goes around comes around.

81. Connect with the Alpha Fee. How can you work together effectively in a way that you can both win and where you are not viewed as a threat? Help her shine, praise her support in public (only if she has supported you, even a little). Remember, praising a lie feels odd, and she will become paranoid, thinking you are manipulating her.

82. Mind your own business. Avoid falling into her trap of becoming her manipulated subject. This will help you keep everybody's respect.

83. Do not plot to bring the Alpha Fee Bee down. She doesn't need your help, thank you very much, and will do this very well on her own.

84. Men and women: we are of the same species. Our brains may be different, but we have complimentary qualities. Let's bring them together.

85. You scratch my back, I'll scratch yours. Let's find win-win opportunities.

86. Find talents at work and bring them forward. It is okay for men to have a more mathematical mind and for women to have more expressive talents. Create opportunities to integrate these abilities for the greater good.

87. Read maps AND ask for directions. The point is getting where you need to go with the least possible roadblocks.

88. This isn't the battle of the sexes. Team up! We're all working together.

89. Want a successful marriage? Want meaningful interpersonal relationships at work? Want successful alliances? Work at it! Just like money doesn't grow on trees, successful relationships don't happen overnight.

90. Maximize your power of alliance, mediation, and collaboration.

91. Train your pups well; lead by example.

92. For men: don't let Alpha Fee Bees walk all over you. We know many Alphas have abused their power. Show you have a backbone. It's the only way to create respect.

93. For women: remember your femininity! We don't need to cut our hair like men and wear androgynous outfits. It's okay to look fabulous and still kick tail!

94. Seek help. If you are an unhappy Alpha who projects all fault and evil to others, seek change.

95. Decide whether you will benefit from medical help, psychological, coaching, mentoring, or all of the above. Take action! It is not a sign of weakness to seek help. It is a sign of weakness to ignore your feelings of weakness.

96. It could be that one person is plotting against you, maybe two... but all of them? If one person does not like you, it's okay, if many don't like you, that may be okay too. But if you justify everybody hating you, chances are, it's not them but you! In general, if this is the case, even you may not like yourself. Become your best friend.

97. Establish alliances to win, not plots to overthrow.

98. Become strong by your own deeds, not by finding fault

in or weakening others. Discover what you have to offer to the world.

99.   Focus on bringing good services and deeds to the world. This should be your driving force.

100. Avoid high emotion in making any personal, professional, or business decisions, particularly if these will likely impact on others (meaning most of your decisions).

101. Train others to become better than you have ever been. Allow yourself to experience the joy of having the apprentice outdo the master. After all, they're only that good because you helped them get there.

102. Use your position of power when you need to call the shots during times of crisis or during times of chaos. Otherwise, encourage open communication and participation of your team.

103. Use joy as your barometer and the friendships and respect from others that you have generated in your path. Nurture the positive attributes of a powerful leader.

104. If you're spending more of your time trying to be liked by others or plotting to overthrow others from their positions, shift to spending more time on getting your own job done.

105. Form strong alliances with those who share your vision and goals. Avoid promoting others based solely on gender or other demographic issues (this goes for

men too!).

106. Stay true to yourself. Don't jump on the bandwagon! Remember that you are a powerful Alpha Female and if no one else will state the obvious problem, then it is your job to guide the pack.

107. Just like love and hate are different manifestations of the same spectrum, positive and negative Alpha Females are polarized expressions of the same strong female leader. As in alchemy, negative can be transformed into positive. If you believe that you can strive for this power of transformation, then there is nothing to stop you from becoming the best Positive Alpha Female that you can be.

GLOSSARY

Alpha Fee: Alpha Fees are strong, positive leaders who enjoy being in charge yet are great team-players and enjoy establishing win-win situations. They appreciate good challenges and strive to win by doing their best. They mind their own business and have consistently advanced in their position of power. Their battles are fair: they win out of their own merit. Both men and women respect these alphas, as they know they will always bring the greater good to the center of focus rather than any personal gain.

Alpha Fee Bee: Alpha Fee Bees seem to be strong on the outside but they are weak on the inside. They are negative leaders who enjoy being in charge for fear of being in someone else's charge. Many Alpha Fee Bees believe they are good leaders, yet they don't work well with others and boycott initiatives where others will shine, even if the initiative will benefit the organization. They always try to secure their position of power and prefer to win alone rather than everybody win. They fear good challenges and strive to win by attacking their opponents' weaknesses.

Alpha Fee IT: Alpha Female Leader in Training

Alpha Female: Alpha Females are female leaders of their pack, whether their pack is family, a team, or an organization.

Alpha Male: Alpha Males are male leaders of their pack, whether their pack is family, a team, or an organization.

Alpha Wannabe: Anyone wanting to become an Alpha

male or female leader.

Delta Dogs: Delta dogs are followers. In this case, I refer to both men and women followers of the Alpha Female leader.

Silent Assassin: The Silent Assassin is an Alpha Fee Bee attempting to destroy her competitor by spreading gossip, backstabbing, or other despicable ways of winning the game.

Superwoman: The Superwoman is a woman who strives to be at her best game at work and at home. She tries to do it all.

GABRIELA CORÁ, MD, MBA

D r. Gaby Corá is President and founder of **The Executive Health & Wealth Institute**®, Inc. She is author of *Leading under Pressure*®: *Strategies to Maximize Peak Performance & Productivity while Maximizing Health & Wellbeing*, **Managing Work in Life**®, and **Quantum Wellbeing**. Dr. Corá is a corporate consultant, life and business coach, licensed medical doctor, board certified psychiatrist, trained mediator, and she has a master's in business administration.

Her energized enthusiasm, strategic focus, and innovative style are qualities in action as a corporate consultant, executive coach, and expert speaker, making her a key collaborator of Fortune 500 companies and international organizations. Dr. Corá works with entrepreneurs, executives, road warriors, professionals, and their organizations, assisting them in leadership, strategic planning, and health & wellness in the workplace.

She has consulted and given presentations in North and South America, Europe, Africa, and Asia. She integrates a unique combination of capabilities: a strong foundation of knowledge, 20 years of experience, and an intuitive deductive ability. She's in the Board of Directors of the American Psychiatric Foundation and an appointed member of the American Psychiatric Association national Committee on Business Relations.

She lectures at the School of Business at University of Miami, she's a Professional Member of the National Speakers Association, and she is a regular guest on radio and television shows speaking on health and wellness. A sought-out expert, she has been featured in *The New York Times, Women Entrepreneur, Smart Money, Money News at News Max, Human Resource Executive, CNN, Fox, Univision, and Telemundo.*

Prior to EH&WI, she was Director, Regional Medical Research Specialist, at Pfizer Pharmaceuticals, serving as the Southeast Regional Council Coordinator and its representative to the sales department. Throughout her career at Pfizer, she was deeply involved in facilitating strategic business planning, effective teambuilding, mentoring, and coaching others individually and in teams, receiving the 2000 Pfizer Values in Action Award for Teamwork.

Prior to Pfizer, she was a Clinical Research Associate at the prestigious National Institutes of Health, serving as Lieutenant Commander in the US Public Health Service, where she was elected Chair of the Hispanic Officers' Advisory Committee to the Surgeon General. As a clinical researcher, she headed the Obsessive-Compulsive Disorder

Unit Research Clinic, building a highly specialized clinical team and conducting state-of-the-art clinical research, which resulted in cutting-edge treatment options and peer-reviewed publications. She received the Hannah Cashman Memorial Award in recognition for her dedicated and compassionate care given by the Consultation Liaison service at NIMH.

Dr. Corá pursued a research career after her residency in Psychiatry at Saint Elizabeths' Hospital, in Washington, DC. Dr. Corá became a doctor at the age of twenty-four in 1989, graduating with a nine month-old and a twenty-five month-old, with honors. She built a successful professional career while she built her personal family life with her husband and children. She is fluent in English, Spanish, and French and appears in *Who's Who in Executives & Professionals, Who's Who in Medicine and Healthcare, Who's Who in America, and Who's Who in the World.*

ADDITIONAL WORK BY DR. GABY CORÁ

LEADING UNDER PRESSURE®

Strategies to Maximize Peak Performance & Productivity while Maximizing Health & Wellbeing

Millions around the world are thinking, planning, and scheming about how to stretch a 24-hour day into an endless and productive workday. Many face the daily quandary of finding new ways to thrive in order to achieve higher goals, with increased competition, progressively limited resources, and the same manpower. Burnt-out, energy-depleted, or constantly stressed, many find themselves unable to take pleasure in their hard-earned position.

Leading under Pressure® will assist you:

- Identify your situation in the Wellbeing and Stress
- Identify your Pressure Points to lead more effectively in times of crisis
- Implement effective strategies to maximize your Peak Performance and Productivity while Maximizing Health & Wellbeing

www.ExecutiveHealthWealth.com

MANAGING WORK IN LIFE®

A Seven Step Plan to Achieve Your Goals and Master Your New Life Business Plan®

If we lived in an ideal world, we would live by the rule of thirds. First, we would work eight hours of the day. Next, we would spend eight hours in recreational activities. Last, but not least, in the ideal world, we would recover our energy by sleeping eight hours every night, refreshing our bodies and minds, to start a new day with plenty of energy and stamina.

Managing Work in Life® will assist you:

- Understand the Myth of Life-Work Balance
- Learn about the Healthy Individual and the Healthy Organization
- Learn a Seven Step Plan to achieve your goals while integrating your plan

www.ExecutiveHealthWealth.com

QUANTUM WELLBEING™

Discover Your Source of Energy:

Create a Strong Core to

Enjoy Enduring Success

A groundbreaking program that integrates Dr. Corá's years of experience as a medical doctor and business consultant, **QUANTUM WELLBEING I:** *The Core*, is the first in the series of meditation and relaxation exercises available for busy executives, road warriors, and entrepreneurs. Dr. Corá facilitates *The Core* using progressive relaxation techniques and guided imagery as you **discover your source of energy: creating a strong core to enjoy enduring success. Quantum Wellbeing** will enhance your health and wellbeing at the deepest level.

When can I use Quantum Wellbeing?

- When you are experiencing high levels of stress
- When you are having trouble sleeping
- When you feel worried about flying
- When you are extremely tired and ready for a nap but need to keep going with work
- When you want your body to relax but your mind to stay focused

www.ExecutiveHealthWealth.com

The New Life Business Plan®

Please visit: **www.ExecutiveHealthWealth.com** for more information about:

- **Leading under Pressure®**
- **Managing Work in Life®**
- **Quantum Wellbeingtm**
- **The New Life Business Plan®**

CORPORATE CONSULTING SERVICES

Dr. Gaby Corá has assisted executives and entrepreneurs, their teams, and their organizations in a wide range of events. She is expert in assessing, diagnosing, planning, and creating intervention plans in complex situations, including crisis leadership, strategic planning, organizational behavior, health and wellness in the workplace, and work in life management. She has extensive experience coaching entrepreneurs and C-level executives.

Although each of her programs has a blueprint representing its core, she thrives to design and custom-make programs that are uniquely applicable to her clients' needs. Her forte is to offer integrated coaching and seminars at your corporation or designated location for your convenience.

Dr. Gaby Corá prefers to conduct the first consultation in person as she firmly believes nothing beats a face-to-face meeting. Your preference may be to see her at her Miami offices or you may both decide it is best for her to see you in action within your organization. She offers in-person and teleconference consultations and she will travel to join you and your team.

Executive Coaching: Individual and Team Coaching

- Leadership Coaching, Mentoring, and Advising
- Performance and Development Coaching
- Crisis Management Coaching

Seminars & Keynotes

- Leading under Pressure®
- Managing Work in Life®
- Quantum Wellbeingtm
- The New Life Business Plan®
- Health & Wellness in the Workplace

EXECUTIVE COACHING

- Comprehensive Individual Assessment
- Individual Coaching
- Group Coaching

INDIVIDUAL COACHING PACKAGES

- COACHING I: 6 Sessions/year.
  - o Assessment at baseline and follow-up on days 30, 60, 90, 180 and 360.

- COACHING II: 13 Sessions/year.
  - o Assessment at baseline and follow-up on days 30, 60, 90, 120, 150, 180, 210, 240, 270, 300, 330, 360 or assessment at baseline and follow-up on days 7, 14, 21, 30, 45, 60, 75, 90, 120, 180, 270, 360.

- COACHING III: 18 Sessions/year.
  - o Assessment at baseline and days 7, 14, 21, 30, 45, 60, 75, 90, 120, 150, 180, 210, 240, 270, 300, 330, 360.

CORPORATE PROGRAMS: Estimated for a group of 25 attendees.

Time 0: Baseline
Time 1: 30 days
Time 2: 60 days
Time 3: 90 days
Time 6: 180 days
Time 12: 360 days

- **PROGRAM I:** Seminars and Group Coaching
  - o Includes an initial, 8-hour workshop at time 0 and a follow-up workshop the following year at time 12, for a total of 2 workshops.
  - o Monthly calls at times 1, 2, 3 and 6 in groups of 5 to 10. For a group of 25, divided in 5 groups of 5 for a 90-minute group-coaching conference call (total of 5 calls at times 1, 2, 3 and 6); or two groups of 10-13 for a 3-hour   group-coaching conference call (total of 2 calls at times 1, 2, 3 and 6).
  - o Ongoing research measures to track progress.
  - o Brief consultations via phone/email as needed at no charge.
  - o Feedback and recommendations.

- **PROGRAM II:** Seminar Series
  - o Includes an initial, 8-hour workshop at time 0, and then 5 additional follow-up workshops (6-hour interactive workshops at times 1, 2, 3 and 6) and an 8-hour workshop at time 12: total of 6 workshops).
  - o Ongoing research measures to track progress.

- o Brief consultations via phone/email as needed at no extra charge.
- o Feedback and recommendations.

- **PROGRAM III:** Seminars and Intensive Group Coaching
  - o Includes an initial, 8-hour workshop at time 0, and a follow-up workshop at time 12, for a total of 2 workshops.
  - o Monthly calls at times 1 through 11 (total of 11), in groups of 5 to 10. For a group of 25, divided in 5 groups of 5 for a 90-minute group-coaching conference call (total of 5 calls at times 1 through 11); or two groups of 10-13 for a 3-hour group-coaching conference call (total of 2 calls at times 1 through 11).
  - o Ongoing research measures to track progress.
  - o Brief consultations via phone/email as needed at no extra charge.
  - o Feedback and recommendations.

To contact Dr. Gaby Corá, to visit her blog, or for more information about Dr. Gaby Corá's resources and services, please visit us at http://www.ExecutiveHealthWealth.com

Gabriela Corá, MD, MBA, President

The Executive Health & Wealth Institute®, Inc

Tel: 305-762-7632 – Toll Free: 1-866-762-7632

WWW.EXECUTIVEHEALTHWEALTH.COM

www.ingramcontent.com/pod-product-compliance
Lightning Source LLC
Chambersburg PA
CBHW052043270326
41931CB00012B/2615